Pie Corbett's Poetry Spine

The best poetry to share with your class!

"The aim is to develop an inclination towards poetry with its joys of surprise, emotion, music and beauty."

Find out more at www.scholastic.co.uk/piecorbett

SCHOLASTIC

Published in the UK by Scholastic Education, 2020
Book End, Range Road, Witney, Oxfordshire, OX29 0YD
A division of Scholastic Limited
London – New York – Toronto – Sydney - Auckland
Mexico City – New Delhi – Hong Kong

SCHOLASTIC and associated logos are trademarks and/or registered trademarks of Scholastic Inc.
www.scholastic.co.uk

© 2020, Scholastic Ltd

123456789   0123456789

British Library Cataloguing-in-Publication Data
A catalogue record for this book is available from the British Library.

ISBN 978-1407-18348-0
Printed by Ashford Colour Press

All rights reserved. This book is sold subject to the condition that it shall not, by way of trade or otherwise, be lent, hired out or otherwise circulated without the publisher's prior consent in any form of binding or cover other than that in which it is published and without a similar condition, including this condition, being imposed upon the subsequent purchaser.

No part of this publication may be reproduced, stored in a retrieval system, or transmitted, in any form or by any means, electronic, mechanical, photocopying, recording or otherwise, other than for the purposes described in the content of this product, without the prior permission of the publisher. This product remains in copyright.

Due to the nature of the web we cannot guarantee the content or links of any site mentioned. We strongly recommend that teachers check websites before using them in the classroom.

Author
Pie Corbett

Editorial
Robin Hunt, Rachel Morgan, Suzanne Holloway, Suzanne Adams

Design
Scholastic Design Team: Dipa Mistry, Andrea Lewis

Typeset
QBS Learning

Photographs
The Quick Brown Fox

Cover Design
Neil Salt

Contents

Introduction	5
Ten ways to establish a poetry climate in schools	7
Reading poetry in school	8
Pie Corbett video support	12
Poetry Spine: **Nursery**	13

- *Dinosaur Roar!*
- *Shark in the Park*
- *The Oxford Treasury of Nursery Rhymes*
- *The Puffin Baby and Toddler Treasury*

Poetry Spine: **Reception**	17

- *My Many Coloured Days*
- *This Little Puffin*
- *Sharing a Shell*
- *A Treasury of Songs*

Poetry Spine: **Year 1**	20

- *Here's a Little Poem*
- *Hey, Little Bug!*
- *When We Were Very Young*
- *The Puffin Book of Fantastic First Poems*

Poetry Spine: **Year 2**	24

- *The Works Key Stage 1*
- *A First Poetry Book*
- *Crazy Mayonnaisy Mum*
- *Heard it in the Playground*

Contents

Poetry Spine: Year 3   27
- *Paint Me a Poem*
- *Quick, Let's Get out of Here*
- *The World's Greatest Space Cadet*
- *The Puffin Book of Utterly Brilliant Poetry*

Poetry Spine: Year 4   30
- *Deep in the Green Wood*
- *Hot Like Fire*
- *Hello H_2O*
- *Sensational!*

Poetry Spine: Year 5   34
- *Lost Magic*
- *The Magic Box*
- *Juggling with Gerbils*
- *The Works 4*

Poetry Spine: Year 6   38
- *Collected Poems for Children (Causley)*
- *New and Collected Poems for Children (Duffy)*
- *Collected Poems for Children (Hughes)*
- *The Works Key Stage 2*

Introduction

The *Poetry Spine* offers a core selection of the best poetry to share with your class.

This spine provides schools with four core poetry books for each year, from Nursery to Year 6. Starting with early nursery and traditional rhymes, the children build up familiarity with many different poets ranging from classical to modern. The spine is cumulative in so far as the poetry becomes increasingly challenging so that by Year 6 children are ready to tackle rich and demanding poetry as, over time, they will have built up confidence, appreciation and knowledge of poetic writing.

As a school, agree on and resource your poetry spine with key anthologies, poets and poems for each term. My *Poetry Spine* should be treated as an initial collection, as you will want to ensure that each year also has many other poetry books, especially by the key poets. Most year groups have three collections from key poets and one core anthology. The purpose of the spine is for children to increasingly become familiar with different poets. It will gradually increase their stamina through familiarity with poetry as a part of their daily reading diet. The *Poetry Spine* is primarily for the daily 'read aloud' programme – whether that be chanting 'The farmer's in his den' or listening to Kit Wright's 'The Magic Box'.

Poem of the week

Establish a 'Poem of the week' in EYFS and Key Stage 1 so that the children have acquired a solid bank of about 100 poems by the time they reach the end of Year 2. At Key Stage 2, establish a 'Poem of the day' to ensure that children hear lots of poetry. You may read the poems to the children or have one child per day read a poem that they have chosen to read to the class.

For working on in class, as part of your English programme, first choose a worthwhile poem. Much of the poetry published over the last twenty years is easy to understand and, while the poems might be fun to read, their impact will be brief. Poems for use in lessons should be worth spending time with: they have to earn their place. In *The Works Key Stage 1* and *The Works Key Stage 2* (Macmillan Poetry), I collected all the poems that I would wish for teaching (organised by year group in the index).

Introduction

Collections and anthologies

Supplement the *Poetry Spine* by gathering other books by poets being studied, as well as a rich range of poetry collections. Some of the poets have their own websites or blogs[1]. The annual CLiPPA poetry award provides a good starting point, listing poetry collections and teaching ideas as well film clips of performances (https://www.clpe.org.uk/poetryline/clippa). Ask for suggestions on Twitter; loiter in bookshops. Supplement this by listening to poets reading their work aloud using the 'Poetry Archive'[2] where you can hear poems read by individual poets.

I have included a core anthology for each year so that children experience a broad range. Ensuring that children have poetry read to them on a regular basis over the years increases the children's familiarity with poetry's many possibilities. The ability to enjoy the challenge of Ted Hughes in Year 6 is gradually built through constant engagement with an increasingly demanding range of poems.

Many of the poems will benefit from discussion or lend themselves to choral performances, and others act as models for writing. Some can be experienced in silence while others may benefit from performance, dance, art or music or be explored through writing. Poems are experiences and they will not always submit themselves to interrogation. Before sharing with the class, please read the poems to make sure that the themes and language are suitable. Those interested in teaching approaches could look at *Jumpstart Poetry* (Routledge) where I write about teaching the reading and writing of poems.[3] ∎

> **Poems are experiences and they will not always submit themselves to interrogation.**

[1] Brian Moses publishes many writing ideas online: www.brian-moses.blogspot.co.uk.
[2] Visit www.childrens.poetryarchive.org
[3] Roger Stevens' Poetry Zone is also a fabulous teaching resource: www.poetryzone.co.uk

Ten ways to establish a poetry climate in schools

- Display poems around the classroom and school – in staff rooms, on the backs of doors, on notice boards.

- As a school, decide to read a 'poem a day'. Have a 'poet of the week', or each term focus every class on a different poet.

- Include a poem in all assemblies.

- Create a 'poet tree' that has different branches for different types of poem and for poets. For example, the haiku branch or the Charles Causley branch. On the leaves, the children copy lines, verses or poems.

- 'Desert Island Poems': read out your favourites and explain what it is you like about each poem.

- 'Poem Swap': find a poem you like and exchange with a friend.

- Put poems onto cards: children then take a poetry card home. Favourites can be learned by heart or performed.

- Record a poetry programme – or ask pupils to prepare a PowerPoint™ of poems transposed onto images or photos.

- Start all staff meetings with a poem.

- Ask each teacher to send a poem as a message to another teacher every Friday morning for a term!

Reading poetry in school

Good poems are experiences and, like music, they may not be readily understood. It is the conjunction between the sound of the poem, its music, and the meaning of the words that creates an effect. The poem creates echoes of meaning for each reader: words triggering memories, images, ideas and emotions.

I remember years ago hearing John Agard reading William Blake's 'The Tyger'. A woman in the audience cried and, later, I asked her why. 'It was like hearing the Earth speak to me,' she said.

To understand a poem, we have to actively engage so that the reader recreates the poem inside their minds, making it their own by relating it to their real and imagined experience. As suggested, poems have to be read aloud to experience the sound of the words and the musicality of the lines. The written poem is like a musical score that can only come alive when the poem is spoken aloud, so this has to be our starting point. Because many poems do not always yield an obvious meaning immediately, loiter with the poem, talking about it, testing the lines aloud. Discuss preferences, parts that resonate, what it seems to be saying and how it is doing that. Let the children tease away at the poem, enjoying its mystery as much as the parts that seem more obvious. Be ready to say *Yes, I'm not sure about what that bit means but it sounds good!*

To be experienced by the children, the poem must be read aloud both by the teacher and, most importantly, by the children. Only through reading a poem or listening to it being read can you feel the experience. The first encounter with a poem may be through a teacher reading to the class or putting the children into groups to prepare a choral reading. As the groups work together, they will naturally begin to try and interpret the poem, thinking about how it should be spoken. The key is to 'vary' pace, rhythm, expression and volume in relation to meaning. Capture performances and create class CDs or film clips; perform for other classes or in assembly. We may never fully understand Blake's 'The Tyger' but we can have it by heart and love the mystery. Bring poems alive with great reading and do not be afraid to use percussive instruments to provide a simple backing or to use illustration or film to enrich the experience. Make the poem live. The more poetry lives fearlessly, the more the children will love poetry without fear.

Poetry comprehension

Discussion is essential, as it is through talk that we may begin to bring into being what we think about a poem. It helps if the teacher models 'thinking aloud' about a poem: what has drawn them to a poem, which bits they enjoy, what aspects 'speak' to their experience.

Share, too, the mysteries or parts of each poem that are hard – these can be put to one side, remaining uncertain at the moment. Explain what interests or surprises. Talk about the word choices and imagery; the pictures a poem paints; the memories or ideas that it triggers; as well as the patterns that add to the pleasure and meaning.

Exploratory and tentative 'book talk' helps a class to grow in understanding and deepens appreciation. Trigger the discussion with an open question such as *What can we say about this?* Then show an authentic interest in the poem and what the children say, relinquishing control over the meaning and helping the class focus and deepen their understanding. Coax out initial ideas, including what the class enjoyed or what the poem made them think about or feel. Remember there is no 'wrong answer', just their thinking. If the comments leave the poem behind or become 'wild', get the children to back up their ideas by referring to the poem. Children read and come up with ideas and then, through discussing and listening to other people's ideas, gradually the class deepens their understanding of what a poem might offer. Slow the pace of discussion and use 'line-by-line' reading to help the children tie clues together and gradually build up the movement through the poem.

Interact with poems

Help children dig under the skin of a poem, with some form of interactive activity:

- Try missing out the title – the children read the poem and then decide in pairs or threes what it might be called and provide evidence for their thinking.
- Cut up a poem by words, lines or verses and challenge the children to reassemble the poem.
- Omit key words from a poem, creating a cloze procedure; the children have to fill in the blanks thinking about rhythm, meaning and style.
- Rewrite a poem as prose and ask the children to then put the poem back into lines, considering where each line or verse break might fall.
- Ask children to illustrate the key image from the poem.

All these activities will encourage children to talk about and engage more deeply with each poem.

Try also using writing as a form of response. Children could advertise a poem, or write about the poem discussing what they liked or disliked, as well as what intrigued them. Some poems lend themselves to writing in role as a character or responding with a diary entry, letter or news item about a dramatic event. Set poems to music or percussion, adding movement or dance to the performance, or use illustration.

Reading poetry in school

A possible teaching sequence

All of the activities in the previous pages of the book will encourage children to talk about and engage more deeply with each poem. Poems, though, are not like sums. They can be difficult to understand in the normal sense, but they can always be experienced, rather like music or art. Here is a suggested approach for a lesson or sequence of sessions:

- **Read and perform:** get the children into small groups to perform the poem. They will need to think about varying the volume, pace and expression in relation to the meaning. Poetry has to be read aloud to be genuinely experienced.
- **Activity:** provide an interactive activity to help the children engage very closely with the poem.
- **Line-by-line reading:** read the poem through bit by bit, closely discussing possible responses and meanings. Always go back, re-read and then think about the movement of the meaning across the poem as a whole.

Here is a simple frame for discussion:

Don't torture poems!

The key to turning children on to poetry is to not be overly concerned about children totally understanding a poem. Good poems are not the same as sums. They do not always add up. But we can enjoy them in the same way that we can enjoy music without really understanding why. If you want to turn children off poetry then the simplest way is to read a poem to the class. Get them to find the five similes and the metaphor. Underline the verbs. Then answer ten questions (which, if they do not get right, then helps them to equate poetry with failure). This is how to help children loathe poetry. The aim is, rather, to develop an inclination towards poetry with its joys of surprise, emotion, music and beauty. Try to avoid strapping a poem to a chair and thrashing a meaning from it with the implements of grammatical torture!

A simple frame for discussion	
First ideas	preferences, links to own life or other poems/stories, memories, bewildering parts to be talked about
Line by line	read it through carefully, talking through what each line means
Feelings and thoughts	what does the poem mean to you?
Pictures	describe the image/s that the poem creates
Poem's pattern and techniques	used to create an effect
Final comment	the most memorable aspect
Summarise	go back and read it all through, looking for a movement or development across the whole poem – what is the theme?

Use a poem as a springboard into writing your own

A key method that helps children to appreciate a poem, and to look and read more closely, is through imitating the poem. Certain poems make this invitation obvious. Everyone knows Kit Wright's 'The Magic Box', which provides a skeleton for children's own ideas. A careful reading of this poem will stimulate possibilities and techniques to try out. Writing in homage or imitation helps us to appreciate the original poem. Perhaps it is only really possible to appreciate a sonnet when we have tried to write one.

Listen to Philip Gross's 'Dreams of an Inland Lighthouse-Keeper', available through the children's poetry archive and found in his collection *Off Road to Everywhere* (Salt, 2010), and an earlier version in *The Works Key Stage 2* (Macmillan Poetry, 2014). In the poem, different boats are created such as *'the boat made of stars'*. Here is a Year 6 child writing in response, taking up the invitation to create their own boat made of unusual materials:

The Boat Made of Stardust

The boat made of stardust
floats over the echoing waves
As living stars
Jump on to the boat
Hitching a moonlit ride.
Celestial bodies
Are concealed
Under towering piles of
Silver and gold.
Delicate grains
Hide in cracks
In the floorboards of the boat.
Heavenly particles
Hang from cobweb threads
Like grotesque decorations.
Bejewelled stars
Glisten in the moonlit sky
And reflect on the
Silver studded surface
Of the boat made of stardust.
L.E.R., Year 6

Other poems contain a poetry idea rather than an obvious pattern. For instance, Blake's 'The Tyger' can be viewed as a poem in which the writer talks to animals, asking questions. Here is an example of this idea used by another Year 6 child:

Snail, snail, why are you so frail?
Snail, snail, why do you leave a silvery trail
Wherever you go?
Snail, snail, why do you carry your house
on your hunched back?
Snail, snail, why do you appear when it rains
And everyone else has gone home? ■

Find out more at www.scholastic.co.uk/piecorbett

Pie Corbett video support

> As a teacher, poetry was absolutely at the heart of teaching English for me. Not only do children love hearing poetry, they love reading and performing poetry too.

Pie Corbett, Literacy Expert

In this video, Pie Corbett introduces the Poetry Spine and talks about some of the poets and anthologies included in his core selection including Julia Donaldson, Ted Hughes and Michael Rosen. Pie also suggests simple ways to integrate poetry into every school day.

Watch the video in full now at www.scholastic.co.uk/piecorbett or on YouTube by visiting our scholasticfilmsuk channel.

> A simple way to ensure poetry becomes a regular feature of the curriculum is to establish a 'poem of the day' system. After lunch, a new poem or old favourite is shared by the teacher, a child or a group performing. You can supplement this by listening to poets reading their work. Ensuring that children have poetry read to them on a regular basis over the years increases their familiarity with poetry's many possibilities.

Pie Corbett, Literacy Expert

Discover more videos online

Visit our YouTube channel to find even more videos from Pie Corbett including storytelling performances, reading for pleasure recommendations and practical tips on how to encourage children to develop their writing skills.

Simply visit www.youtube.com/ scholasticfilmsuk to browse our videos.

Nursery

Dinosaur Roar!

Paul Stickland and Henrietta Stickland *(Macmillan)*

This is a small stroke of wonderful, memorable genius. Every so often, a book comes along that hits the spot and this dinosaur rhyming book, endorsed by the Natural History Museum, is an absolute classic. Many snuggly re-readings, looking at the pictures and chanting the rhyme, will draw almost any child into the dinosaur world. The rhyming is perfect and, of course, the children love spotting the different, brilliantly drawn dinosaurs.

Once you have read the rhyme a number of times begin to use the old trick of chanting the rhyme but missing out the rhyme for the children to fill in the gap. As they grow in confidence in putting in the rhymes, you can invite them to join in with the whole thing by saying *Let's say the poem together today*. Use plenty of expression so that you give a gruff *'roar'*, and make your voice sound *'strong'*, *'grumpy'* or *'sweet'* as you read it. Expression helps to give meaning and makes the whole experience of being read to much more engaging. In fact, we could say that children love it when adult readers 'do the voices', though you do have to remember which voice or expression goes with which character! There is plenty to spot on the pages so that the book becomes something to explore together.

You can see the impact of 'Dinosaur Roar!' in this piece of shared writing with Nursery children:

I dreamed I saw
A cat's heart beat,
The biggest book flickering its pages,
The moon sparkling at night,
The point of an iceberg,
A merry-go-round in the distance,
A Tyrannosaurus Rex roaring.

There are other wonderful books in this series and, ideally, you would have a collection of 'dinosaur books'. For instance, *Ten Terrible Dinosaurs* (Macmillan Children's Books) is a superb counting book, which would make an ideal companion to *Dinosaur Roar!* in the classroom. It is lovely and important to have snuggly reading with small children, and that bond between the book, the adult and the story or rhyme is essential; books such as *Dinosaur Roar!* also offer a chance to act out the story and move to it as it is chanted aloud, physically exploring the meaning of the words.

Nursery

Shark in the Park!

Nick Sharratt (*Corgi*)

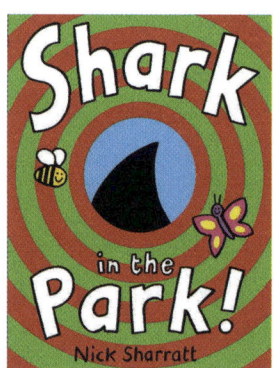

Alongside *Dinosaur Roar!*, *Shark in the Park!* is one of my favourite early rhyming books for Nursery children. There is just something wonderfully scary and funny about the story idea and the tricky illustrations where the shark turns out to be something else. I have often watched Nursery children around a sand tray chanting this story quite independently. The rhythm of the words, *'There's a shark in the park'* seems to stick so rapidly and firmly into children's minds. Perhaps it is the conjunction between the sound of the words and the scariness of sharks, which for many are today's equivalent of the Big Bad Wolf. Nick Sharratt's wonderful illustration of the shark makes it look so scary and nasty enough to send shivers down the spine, but of course the story is quite safe as we can always close the book.

Try exploring the shape of the shark in the park with the children. What might the shark's fin look like? Make a simple list of similes as this nursery class did when they were thinking about what a crescent moon looks like:

The clown's smile is like

A bendy banana,

A nursery rhyme boat,

A hot dog on his face,

A rainbow upside down.

You will want to set up a play area where the book sits in residence and there are toys so that the children can pretend read and play at the story. In this way, we introduce them to a thing of joy: they learn to sit, listen, concentrate and join in with the experience of a wonderful rhyme; then they can go off and play at the story, becoming storytellers themselves, recycling the language. If the adults make sharing the rhyme together memorable then children will quite naturally want to go away and play at the rhyme, reprocessing the language together. In this way they have a shared experience, which begins to shift them from solitary play into parallel or cooperative play.

Gather together a Nick Sharratt collection so that the children can begin to build a sense of an author/illustrator that they love. This may well be their first step towards developing a taste for a favourite author. *Shark in the Dark!* (Picture Corgi) is a splendid follow-up that follows the same idea and so, too, is *Shark in the Park on a Windy Day!* (Corgi). If you love these books then the children will too. I always enjoy sharing another Nick Sharratt title, *Don't Put Your Finger in the Jelly, Nelly* (Scholastic) and suspect that, because I love this book, my enthusiasm will spread to the children: they learn that reading is one of the great joys of life. In this way, we grow the roots of a 'reading for pleasure' culture, which will last most children for the rest of their lives.

The Oxford Treasury of Nursery Rhymes

Edited by Karen King, Sarah Williams and Ian Beck (Oxford University Press)

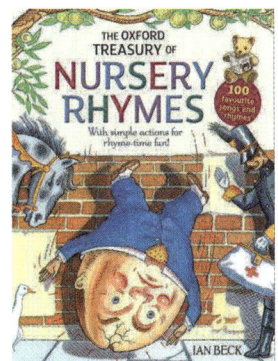

This is an essential book for a nursery, playgroup or mother and toddler group, and ideally every household would have this excellent anthology of over 100 traditional songs and rhymes. There are useful notes and helpful drawings showing actions that can be used to make the rhymes interactive.

Many of these rhymes are ideal for one-to-one sharing sessions with small children and babies as they include knee-jogging rhymes, bouncing rhymes, patting and clapping as well as simple lullabies and rocking rhymes. Early on, a bedrock of interactive rhymes is crucial as a gateway into later development. It is here that children communicate and learn to play together with an adult carer in creating something that is both memorable and pleasurable. It would be worth bringing parents together to teach them early rhymes such as 'This is the Way the Ladies Ride', 'Little Miss Muffett', 'Humpty Dumpty', 'Hickory, Dickory, Dock', 'Hey, Diddle, Diddle' and 'Jack and Jill'. These could be provided on an audio CD for use at home as well as in school or placed onto the relevant website so that parents know how the songs are sung.

No baby or toddler should miss out on the thrill of 'Round and Round the Garden', knowing that the tickle is about to happen. Simple counting rhymes such as 'Five Fat Sausages' are an ideal introduction to counting backwards. The version of 'Incy, Wincy Spider' is provided with simple actions to make it a rhyme that the children can act out. If you were reading *Mr Gumpy's Outing* (Red Fox) then surely you would teach the class 'Row, Row, Row Your Boat' to sing along while pretending to row. I've always had a soft spot for 'Two Fat Gentlemen' and 'Here are Grandma's Spectacles'. Early clapping rhymes such as 'Pat-a-Cake' are essential in helping children to listen attentively and begin to keep a steady beat, clapping or moving in time. There is a strong link between children who can keep a beat and success in early reading!

My personal favourites of these early traditional verses are the singing and dancing rhymes, as it is through this cooperative group endeavour that children learn how to play, sing and move as one with their playmates. Cracking action and circle rhymes include 'Looby-Loo', 'The Grand Old Duke of York', 'Ring-a-Ring o'Roses', 'The Farmer's in His Den' and the joys of 'Five Little Speckled Frogs', as well as the ubiquitous 'The Wheels on the Bus', which can be varied endlessly to suit the circumstances. What joys to share, and as time is always limited it would be worth talking this through with the Reception teachers locally to decide which songs and rhymes will be taught in which year group.

Nursery

The Puffin Baby and Toddler Treasury

(Puffin)

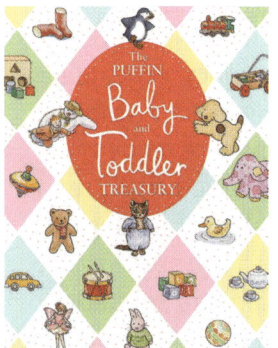

This is a lovely book that blends poems, rhymes and old stories such as Beatrix Potter's *The Tale of Tom Kitten* alongside newer classics such as *The Snowman* and *Spot's First Picnic*. It is illustrated by a wide variety of our best illustrators for the very young.

There are the expected thumping songs such as 'Old Macdonald', which is an absolute staple for nursery children especially, as it is easy to innovate upon and make up new verses. 'If You're Happy and You Know it' fits into the same vein as an adaptable little piece of joy for which children can suggest new ideas and therefore gain confidence. Older rhymes such as 'Here We Go Round the Mulberry Bush' provide an opportunity for singing in a circle and gently moving around. This ancient rhyme is closely related to 'Gathering Nuts in May' and they form a part of our tradition. It's not really necessary for the children to understand every word but they should meet these songs and rhymes, as they are a part of our shared culture and history. 'The Owl and the Pussy-Cat' is the most common poem that infant children know. Hopefully, the *Poetry Spine* will introduce them to a richer diet, even though this poem is unique and wonderful.

The stories include 'The Three Little Pigs', 'Goldilocks and the Three Bears', 'The Three Billy Goats Gruff' and 'The Gingerbread Man'. These are ideal retellings full of rhythm that suggest that the authors have retold them many times to ensure that their retellings read aloud effectively and easily, with flow.

Get the children joining in with the stories so that they increasingly develop the ability to listen, keep still, join in with and enjoy being read to. It's worth remembering that many children – possibly as many as 50% – will not be read to at home or know any rhymes, other than perhaps a jingle from an advert, on entry to an Early Years setting.

Counting rhymes are a good starting point – though avoid using rhyme as it is very difficult. You could instead have objects in a bag to help get ideas as this Nursery group did:

Five huge giants.

Four funny foxes.

Three yellow bananas.

Two tiny tigers.

One grey mouse.

Reception

My Many Coloured Days

Dr Seuss (*Red Fox*)

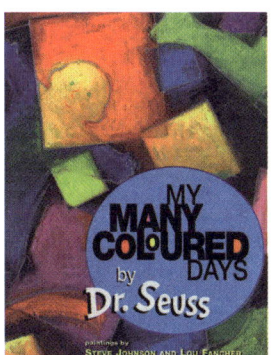

Small children all pass through a phase of alighting on a favourite book, which they like to hear again and again. Through constant repetition, they actually learn the text word for word and thus begins the journey towards becoming a reader – loving a favourite text and growing in confidence by 'joining in' with the reading, and beginning to feel like a reader. This little book is the right size for little hands. It is just right in terms of wear and tear and will last many re-readings. The text associates colours with moods and makes a wonderful introduction to talking about how our feelings vary. It is also an absolute standby for introducing basic colours and could be used for simple artwork in school as well as for colour mixing and experimentation.

While the pictures are simple enough, there is plenty to discuss. The images reflect the moods but the font is also used to suggest feelings. Read and re-read with the class, small groups or for snuggly one-to-one reading. The colour work could be used to create a wall display or floor book based on different colours and how they make us feel, as well as for painting different animals which have strong colours. I'd also want to link this with the *Elmer* books!

Make up some magical wishes using different colours and feelings. Here are some children's own 'funny' ideas:

I wish I was a brown owl called WOL.

I wish I was a red slipper covered in mud.

I wish I was a buzzing bee that stings like yellow lightning.

I wish I was a white duck with a magic beak that made spells.

I wish I was a thief creeping in the backyard waiting to steal the golden yachts out of the sea.

Dr Seuss has something quirky, memorable and magical about his books. He is the absolute master of rhyme and wordplay and should be a staple part of every small child's early repertoire, so make sure that you have a collection of other Dr Seuss titles for enjoyable reading. The early importance of re-reading favourites cannot be underestimated as it is through this activity that children not only begin to love books and build a sense of taste for different books that they enjoy, but also begin to grow in confidence with the whole experience of early reading. It's extraordinary to think that *The Cat in the Hat* came out in 1957. Dr Seuss has stood the test of time. I'd also buy in *Green Eggs and Ham, The Cat in the Hat Comes Back, Fox in Socks* and *How the Grinch Stole Christmas!* for starters. In that way, the class can begin to get the feel for a poet, attune their ears to rhyme and sound within words and learn that books and reading can be a funny and highly enjoyable part of life.

Reception

This Little Puffin

Compiled by Elizabeth Matterson (*Puffin*)

When I started teaching, every teacher working at Key Stage 1 or in the Early Years went out on their first teaching practice clutching a copy of *This Little Puffin*. Anyone working with small children should at the very least have a few songs and rhymes that children can join in with, as well as some interactive stories to tell.

The book provides a huge bank of rhymes, often with simple instructions for actions so that everyone can join in. Occasionally there are simple illustrations for slightly more complex hand movements as well as music to provide a simple tune. Reception children should be experiencing rhyme and song as a daily, systematic part of their curriculum. This binds the class together and helps children learn to sit, listen and join in. At first they may just listen but gradually will start to join in with actions, calling out the end of line rhymes and choruses. Through constant revisiting of favourites, they build up an ever-increasing repertoire of songs and rhymes. In this way, the early roots of our culture are passed on, which draws us all together as we have the same imaginative bank of shared literary experiences.

We know, too, that children who are attuned to hearing rhyme find reading and spelling easier because of analogy. Early work on sound and rhyme helps children to discriminate sounds and begins to lay the foundation for phonemic awareness. For this new edition, the original editor went back out to ask schools, nurseries and playgroups, as well as mother and toddler groups, for their favourite songs and rhymes. Some of the rhymes are variations and innovations on well-known songs, showing how teachers and children often adapt the familiar to create something new and make a rhyme their own. This anthology is an absolute gem and should be in every Early Years teacher's collection, and used on a daily basis.

Sharing a Shell

Julia Donaldson (*Macmillan*)

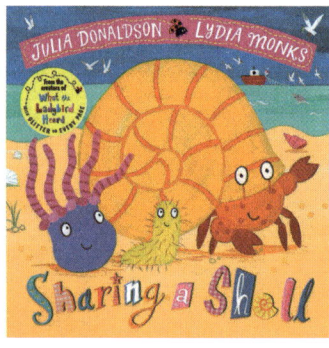

It would be useful to collate a list of core rhyming books for Nursery, Reception and Year 1 children to experience. For instance, *Each Peach Pear Plum* by Janet and Allan Ahlberg (Puffin), *Who Sank the Boat?* by Pamela Allen (Picture Puffin), *My Cat Likes to Hide in Boxes* by Eve Sutton (Picture Puffin), *Oi Frog!* by Kes Gray and Jim Field (Hodder), *Hairy Maclary from Donaldson's Dairy* by Lynley Dodd (Puffin), *Don't Forget the Bacon!* by Pat Hutchins (Red Fox) and *Ten in the Bed* by Penny Dale (Walker Books) might well feature in such a list for any Reception class.

I would want to add in a second 'poet' alongside Dr Seuss, the wonderful rhymester and storyteller Julia Donaldson. Already, *The Gruffalo* (Macmillan) has become a classic that every child knows, and rightfully so, because both the rhyming and the illustrations have created an enduring tale. My favourite Julia Donaldson books would include *Tiddler* (Scholastic), *Room on the Broom* (Macmillan), *The Snail and the Whale* (Macmillan), *Stick Man* (Scholastic), *A Squash and a Squeeze* (Macmillan) and *The Smartest Giant in Town* (Macmillan). The stories can be sung, chanted, acted out, drawn and played with independently. Have a special month when you read and re-read the books, leaving copies for children to dip into and read.

Every school has the main classics mentioned above but *Sharing a Shell* is less well known. To put together the *Poetry Spine*, I asked many teachers and this one came up as a favourite for one headteacher who not only loved the illustrations and the rhythm of the story, but also the values that underpin the tale. One of the key things that many children have to learn as they come into school will be the simplest but sometimes the hardest of things – how to share when perhaps we do not want to, and how to make friends.

A Treasury of Songs

Julia Donaldson (*Macmillan*)

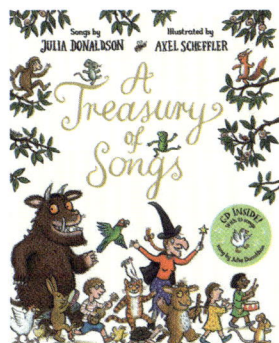

Poetry and rhymes are an important part of early literacy but so, too, are songs. Singing helps to make language memorable. Think about the thousands of songs that you know word for word. We would never have been able to learn such large amounts of text without the musical element. This treasury comes with a CD so that you can hear how the songs should be sung, join in and share with your class.

Julia Donaldson once busked around France and Italy, so her singing roots go back a long way. I heard her once talking at a World Literacy Day event. She spent about five minutes telling us why reading mattered and then halted. With a gleam in her eye, she then began to get us singing her stories and acting them out. We created movements for and about three stories, rehearsing and then performing for ourselves, singing with gusto. By the end of that, there was no need for her to explain why the story mattered. We had experienced the most satisfying, memorable pleasure and the stories had literally been brought alive.

As long as the teacher is confident with the songs and the words then almost every child will soon pick up on the rhythm and begin to join in, increasingly learning the song. Ideally, each song should have simple actions, which will help to reinforce the meaning. Story maps can be drawn on strips of lining paper so that the class can see what is coming next. Keep any maps very clear so that they are just memory-joggers and not over complicated.

Most of the 23 songs in the book are either stories sung or songs to accompany Donaldson's well-known books. If doing 'Goldilocks and the Three Bears' as a class story, make sure that you also sing 'When Goldilocks came to the house of three bears'. A great source for songs to accompany traditional tales is Kaye Umansky's *Three Singing Pigs* (A&C Black) featuring 'The Little Red Hen', 'Three Little Pigs' and 'The Shoemaker and the Elves' as well as 13 other sung stories and a set of teaching notes.

Rhyming poetry is too hard for most young children but many find a simple, repeated pattern ideal for writing their own lines.

In my magical factory
I would make a bear of bricks,
I would make a bandage of electricity,
I would make a light switch of shirts,
I would make a rainbow of eyes,
I would make a sun of calendars.

Read the anthologies for ideas of things to write about.

Year 1

Here's a Little Poem

Collected by Jane Yolen and Andrew Fusek Peters (*Walker Books*)

This is a lovely book, illustrated by the wonderful Polly Dunbar with wit, zest and great joy. Jane Yolen and Andrew Fusek Peters are the editors, calling on a repertoire of poets from either side of the Atlantic. The book has a larger format, with big font, and this makes it ideal for sharing with a class or group. The tone of the poems is generally upbeat, though there are moments which may lead to deep discussions. It is a book of beauty and joy and an absolute must in the classroom. The poems are well crafted and will read aloud effectively.

The rhymes have a happy disposition, well matched by the exuberant illustrations, and it would be easy enough to reread and reread the collection, a few poems per day. Have copies in the book area so that children can browse, look at the pictures and find favourites that they know through auditory memory and can begin to read for themselves. This form of early 'pretend reading' gives children confidence in their growth as a reader because it makes them feel grown up that they can read, and constant playing at reading is an aspect of becoming a reader.

The editors have a great ear for what will read aloud well and any other collections aimed at the younger age group that are loitering in the school could supplement this anthology. When sharing the poems with the children, it is not necessary that everything be understood. I have seen the experience of being read to killed stone dead by lengthy explanations. The rhythmic experience of the language spoken aloud sometimes works a charm on the children even if everything is not fully understood. Perhaps over time we might tease away at the meaning, but the main thing is for the class to love the experience of the songs and rhymes with their understanding gradually growing.

To start with, try writing simple poems using description and similes about the weather, when reading the section 'I go outside' in *Here's a Little Poem*:

The fog slides down the road
like a grey caterpillar
crawling down a steep hill.

Amanda, 6 yrs

Hey, Little Bug!

James Carter (*Lincoln Children's Books*)

Later on, in Year 3, children will come across James Carter again. He is one of a few modern poets who is able to write effectively and with some care and depth for very young children without resorting to slapstick silliness. The actual reading age of the words means that many Year 1 children will be able to read these to themselves, so a selection for guided reading or the book corner would be useful.

James wrote these poems for his daughters when they were younger, drawing on things that they said and did. When he performs the poems, he uses actions and invites teachers to develop their own actions with the children. The poem, 'Where did we go?' invites the reader to add in new places and would make a great one for children to learn, perhaps adding their own ideas. The poem 'Hands' is a rhyming list of things that hands can do and could be used as a sentence starter for writing other ideas. Make a long list of all the sorts of things that hands can do 'grip', 'grab', 'grasp', 'pull', 'tug', 'stroke', 'wave', 'shove', 'brush', 'point', 'pick' and then model how to extend each idea – but avoid rhyming as it will limit their writing.

The poem 'Listen' is a very simple rhythmic opportunity for choral performance:

Listen to the rhythm
When thunder goes

BOOM!

Listen to the rhythm
When cats go

PURR!

Try adding in other ideas, using actions and sound effects.

'Show and tell' could lead into writing an alphabet poem, using names and extending the sentence to say what each character does:

Alice ran down the longest road.
Boris bought a spicy bun.
Candy read her favourite book.

Use the 'Crayon Poem' to write sentences about what the different colours could be used to draw.

With these crayons
I could draw
An orange sun sinking at night,
A blue sky high above me,
A green field with cows grazing…

This poem would sit well alongside Drew Daywalt's book *The Day the Crayons Quit* (Harper Collins).

Year 1

When We Were Very Young

AA Milne (*Egmont*)

My parents read these to me from a very young age so that I grew up with the rhythms, patterns and images. Of course, they are in many ways very old fashioned but there is no one quite like AA Milne, author of the *Winnie the Pooh* books, for rhyming verse. There are actually two books of verse and I chose this one because it has in it 'The King's Breakfast'. Like many small children I didn't understand everything in the poem but I loved the rhythm and sound of the words – it was like listening to a well-known, comforting song where I could join in with the 'good bits'. I remember being slightly bewildered by why they had to go and see the cow to ask about butter, as I didn't realise that milk was needed to make butter and milk came from cows. But then, my experience of nursery rhymes was that anything could happen in this surreal world – cows could jump over the moon, teapots could speak and farmers lived a den, whatever that was!

I spent some time thinking about whether to include this book because the images and ideas are from a long-forgotten era. But even back when I was a child, we never dressed or lived like the characters portrayed in the illustrations or poems. However, what was memorable and most powerful was the quality of the writing. There is no one else – though Allan Ahlberg comes close – as good at writing for very young children in such a substantial and magical way, with complete control over rhyming verse.

It would be ideal to read some of the *Winnie the Pooh* stories alongside this collection. Many of the poems are ideal for children to join in with and even act out. You'll find in here the reason why you should never walk on the lines in the pavement! Don't be afraid of the gentler rhymes such as 'Missing'.

One practical activity to do with the children might be to make a list of things that make us happy, after reading the poem 'Happiness'. Here is an example:

I like running in the playground
as fast as cheetahs.
I like eating yellow custard
as thick as sweet mud.
I like being with my brother
because he makes me laugh
like a clown.
I like the colour blue
because it is like the sky.

The Puffin Book of Fantastic First Poems

Edited by June Crebin (*Puffin*)

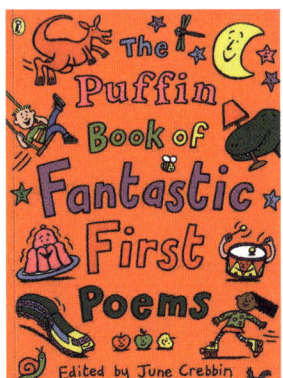

This wonderful collection of poems about animals, playtime, family, food, bedtime, outings, and holidays, as well as nonsense poems, is richly illustrated by various artists. It reminds me of the great anthologies that John Foster published through Oxford University Press, which were colour-illustrated throughout and very popular with children. There is a great mixture of classical as well as modern poems that are ideal for reading aloud, and some for performing as a class.

Pauline Clarke's great poem *'My Name is…'* is a good model for making up new and ridiculous names – just enjoying the language and playing with it!

My name is shark's tooth Peter.
My name is wind in the trees.
My name is ginger pudding.
My name is knobbly knees.

For choral performance there is the wonderful 'Spaghetti! Spaghetti!', 'Rickety Train Ride' and Eleanor Farjeon's 'Cats'. Don't dodge the classic poems by RL Stevenson, Walter de la Mare and Alfred Noyes, who children will meet later on through poems such as 'The Listeners' and 'The Highwayman'. One simple way to learn the poems is for the teacher to re-read during any five-minute pause in the day and invite children to join in as they begin to memorise. We know using actions to go with the meaning can speed this up and, of course, a story map also can act as an effective memory-jogger.

The anthology could be shared over a half term, exploring a section each week. Ideally, have a few copies available for the children to browse through at quiet times, revisiting favourites and re-reading. I think it's important that children may not need to understand every single word. When a poem is sufficiently well crafted, the meaning and music will work their own magic. Careful discussion or the use of images or props may be necessary, but sometimes I think we can enjoy things that we might not necessarily fully understand. June Crebbin's own story-poem 'The Dinosaur's Dinner' is great fun, reads aloud well and could be illustrated by the class, with children taking different sections to create a wall display of the poem.

Year 2

The Works Key Stage 1

Chosen by Pie Corbett (*Macmillan*)

At the back of this anthology, I organise all the poems by year group – Reception, Year 1 and then Year 2.

I begin with the very roots of poetry – traditional nursery rhymes, circle songs, action rhymes – moving into skipping, dipping, clapping and counting rhymes, with a few riddles and tongue twisters. These rhymes and songs are our tradition and lie at the heart of our culture. They could be added to by playground rhymes and early rhymes from other cultures. At the back of the book, I have included instructions for playing the songs and rhymes. The anthology then moves on to poems about ghosts, pirates, aliens as well as fairies, princesses and mermaids. The poems then shift on to exploring feelings, families, as well as animals and the natural world.

There are wonderful poems here to perform: 'Mrs Sprockett's Strange Machine', 'The Engine Driver', 'Quack, said the Billy-goat', 'The Owl and the Pussy-cat'. Also, try simple raps like Brian Moses's 'Hippopotamus Dancing', and don't fight shy of classical poetry like Robert Louis Stevenson's 'Windy Nights', which makes a wonderful assembly performance piece.

List poems like 'In this room', 'Topsy Turvy' and 'Paint' provide simple structures for children's own writing – though remember to gather plenty of ideas and use shared writing to create a class version first. Clare Bevan's poems about fairies, mermaids and princesses often provide simple structures for children's own writing. A Bedtime Rhyme for Young Fairies is a simple counting rhyme. Of course, you could write about goblins, elves, giants, ogres, dragons or trolls instead of fairies! Invent more 'Fairy Names'; write facts; create collective nouns, a rule book, things that can be done; list frightening things as well as what is learned in school. Almost all of her poems make tempting models – though rhyming may constrain so let the children write their ideas without that demand.

After reading the section 'The Animal World', decide which animals might be 'inside of you' and write a list poem using animals or other things:

There is a cat inside of me
that scratches everyone in sight.
There is a page inside of me
that rustles all the time.
There is a name inside of me
that calls 'Peter'.
There is a crow inside of me
that flies around my heart.
There is a fish inside of me
that swims around my blood.
There is a desk inside of me
that keeps all my best ideas.

Emavel, 7 years

A First Poetry Book

Chosen by Pie Corbett and Gaby Morgan (*Macmillan*)

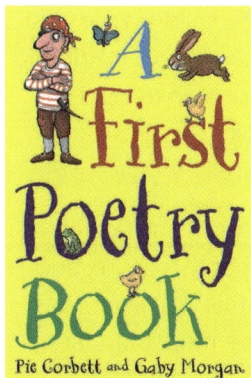

This is another meaty book of poems to read from and let children select poems to perform for the class. When I taught, we held a daily slot for 'poem of the day' and every child had to find a poem, prepare a reading and share it with the class. Sometimes children got together and would perform as a group. We also kept our 'poem of the week' going so that by the end of the year, they knew well a bank of over 30 poems.

Leave a few copies of this anthology in the book corner so that children can re-read favourites, copy them out if they wish and illustrate for a display. Modern technology means that it is now simple to put together audio clips of children reading and performing as well as making films of performances. This does mean that the children can hear how they sound and think about whether their readings have appropriate expression and rhythm. Provide percussive instruments and chime bars for children to use to provide simple tunes and beats to a poem as well as using body percussion.

One of the big issues for children writing poetry at Key Stage 1 is that most of the poems they read will rhyme and yet writing successfully in rhyme is technically too demanding for a young child. However, a poem such as 'Sounds' by Robin Mellor provides a simple format for writing where the ideas matter more than attempting rhyme. An alternative approach is to take the basic idea from a poem such as 'The Quiet Things' by Eric Finney but model how to write a list of quiet things without worrying about rhyme:

These are the quiet things I do:
Watch traffic from my bedroom,
Stare at the cracks in the ceiling,
Read my comics on the floor,
Stroke our cat Choco as she snoozes,
Draw cartoons of pirate ships,
Stand in the playground and stare out
At the block of flats across the road,
Daydream in my head...

You could also try using a simple repeated phrase. The following is a response to a reading of Moira Andrews' poem 'Imagine the world':

In my dreams I saw
a cunning connoisseur
plotting to blow up the houses of parliament,
a flying crocodile swooping over
the United States of America,
a Norway lobster lying on a dish of enchantment,
a grey and white dusty house
in the land of chaos.

Ted, 7 years

Year 2

Crazy Mayonnaisy Mum

Julia Donaldson (*Macmillan*)

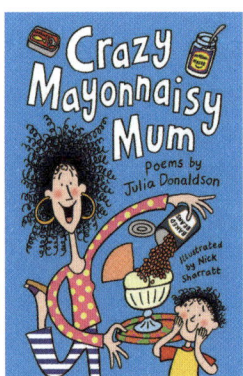

Julia Donaldson is the one of a few highly popular authors that every child knows through such books as 'The Gruffalo', 'A Squash and a Squeeze' and 'Stick Man'. Nick Sharratt, full of wit and fun, illustrates this collection of her poetry.

Many of these poems read aloud as if they were songs and, as Julia Donaldson also writes songs, the boundary is close and it doesn't really matter whether you sing these aloud or perform them as poems. Some of the poems are retellings of traditional tales which would lend themselves to retelling as stories by the children. Begin by getting to know a poem such as 'The Mouse and the Lion'. Then work out with the children the basic plot line and model how to turn it back into a traditional tale. Then let them try the same approach using a poem such as 'The Crow and the Fox', 'The Stork and the Fox' or 'The Tortoise and the Hare'.

This collection might well last half a term and you could get the children to give each poem a score, add these up and create an average. In this way favourites could be identified and ultimately the most popular poem learned chorally using a map and actions before performing in assembly. Alternatively, the five or six most popular poems could be learned by different groups for a Year 2 'slam'! The rules of the slam involve the poems being performed and then the performances voted on for clarity, expression, movement and rhythm.

Heard it in the Playground

Allan Ahlberg (*Puffin*)

Please Mrs Butler (Puffin) is possibly the most popular poetry collection in primary school and as most schools will have a copy to share, I selected another Ahlberg title, *Heard it in the Playground*. Of course, Allan Ahlberg is well known for the wonderful range of stories, many illustrated by Janet Ahlberg, who illustrated such gems as *The Jolly Postman* and *Peepo* (both Puffin). Fritz Wegner, who manages to catch exactly the right tone for the poems, illustrates this collection.

Allan was a primary school teacher himself but to help him write the poems, he spent time in Inglehurst Junior School, soaking up the atmosphere, observing and seeking out possibilities for poems. The actual poem 'Heard it in the Playground' was specifically written for children to belt out as a performance. The middle section of the book contains five songs. 'The Grumpy Teacher' rollicks along to the tune of 'What Shall We Do with the Drunken Sailor' and would make a wonderful end-of-year performance in a final assembly.

Like the poems in *Please Mrs Butler*, these poems capture the everyday life of school. From wet coats steaming, to registration, to swimming lessons, Ahlberg shows how steeped he is in the life of primary schools. I can imagine he was a good teacher as the poems exude warmth and pleasure in the 'everydayness' of playground games, parents' evenings and 'finishing off'! To my ear, Ahlberg manages to write rhythmically so that the poems flow in the great tradition of writers such as AA Milne. I imagine that he must have spent a lot of time saying the poems aloud as he composed them, to capture such fluid verse. It sounds so easy when we read it aloud but it is so hard to compose. ■

Year 3

Paint Me a Poem

Grace Nichols (*Bloomsbury*)

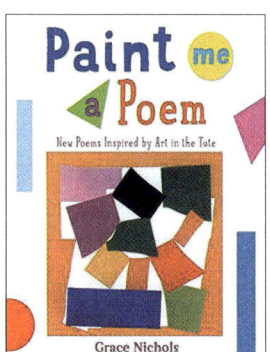

This wonderful book arose from a year-long residency at the Tate Gallery. Grace Nichols wrote poems in response to paintings and sculptures and worked with children from local schools. There are helpful notes at the back about the paintings as well as some excellent ideas for developing children's poetic writing. Each painting has a poem by Grace and many also have children's poems. Ideally, take children to a local gallery so that they can experience the paintings and use them as a focus for writing. If this is not possible, the internet is a rich source of images.

One of my favourite writing workshops involves my postcard collection of works of art. I set out about 40 cards and let everyone choose one that speaks to them. I put on the board an image and use it to model how to write a poem based on the poem. Try using a repeated phrase to create ideas such as *In this world, I can see…*, or make a list of key descriptive details, building a verbal picture of the painting. When publishing the children's writing, get them to carefully draw an image from their chosen painting and use colour to bring it alive so that they produce an illustrated poem.

The following poem came from a workshop in Year 6 at Hanwell Fields Community School in Banbury, and is based on Renoir's wonderful painting *The Umbrellas*.

The sad, pale-faced lady stares;
a puzzled thought enters her confused mind.
Her heavy dress drags;
the straw basket droops.
Umbrellas explode like bats' wings,
like blue waves rising.
A white bonnet rests,
sleeps on Anna's drenched head.
Clutching her wooden hoop,
she wonders in her traumatised mind.

Clare was in Year 6 when she wrote independently this poem based on the image of a painting by Edward Burra titled *The Hand*.

The Poker Room

The knife lies motionless in the murky room.
The hand quivers, a sudden crash,
A streak of lightning stuns the silent sky.
A breeze blown, the cigarette smoke streaks
In a misty haze out through the door.
The table shudders as the stranger reaches
For the dusty gin bottle.
The carved, silent ring presents –
An omen.
A crumpled week old paper
Floats to the ground.
Blurred dots of the dice roll
To show a six.
The stranger cackles,
Startling.

Clare, 10 years

Year 3

Quick, Let's Get out of Here

Michael Rosen (*Puffin*)

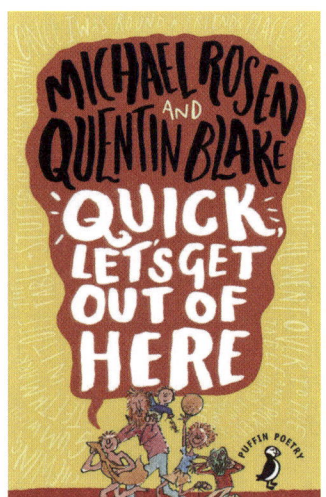

This wonderful book of poems was published back in 1983. It is a classic and has stood the test of time so well because it captures childhood effortlessly and truthfully. Funny, crazy and sometimes sad, this volume introduces us to baby Eddie, Michael's friend Harrybo, as well as his mum, dad and brother. Many of the poems are monologues about family events. Almost every poem could open up a session, with children responding with similar stories and discussing 'times when the same thing happened to me'.

In the main, the poems are free-flowing monologues, so the experience of reading the poems is rather like being with a good friend who has a great store of family stories. Every poem will trigger discussions about what has happened in the poem, but also springboard memories about similar things that have happened. One of the triumphs of the book is that it validates everyday experiences. The book says: *'your own experiences matter and can be the very stuff of poetry'*.

Several of the poems lend themselves to direct imitation such as 'I Know Some Who Can', 'Wise One', or to inventing mad meals and mad drinks. Most will trigger similar anecdotes that can be written in the same free-flowing style, capturing the moment without any need to embellish or use fancy flourishes, which so often falsify experience. Tune children in to noticing the sorts of thing that their family says, gathering family expressions. In the box below are some that my parents often used:

The book contains one of my favourite poems, 'Chocolate Cake', which is a great performance piece. Wonderfully illustrated by Quentin Blake, the images add an affectionate atmosphere as they build a picture of Michael and his family. Check out Michael's website and make sure you have other books of his available such as *You Can't Catch Me!*, *You Wait Till I'm Older Than You* and *Wouldn't You Like to Know* (Puffin). This is literature that takes us right to the heart of the truth of experience.

A bad workman blames his tools.	*No news is good news.*
An apple a day keeps the doctor away.	*No smoke without fire.*
A rolling stone gathers no moss.	*One good turn deserves another.*
Better late than never.	*Out of the frying pan into the fire.*
Don't put all your eggs in the same basket.	*The early bird catches the worm.*
Don't count your chickens before they hatch.	*Two heads are better than one.*
Empty vessels make the most noise.	
Every cloud has a silver lining.	
Let sleeping dogs lie.	
Look before you leap.	

The World's Greatest Space Cadet

James Carter (*Bloomsbury*)

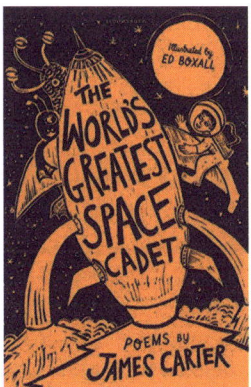

If your school has been using the Poetry Spine for a couple of years then the children will have already met James Carter's poetry in Year 1 with the collection *Hey, Little Bug!* (Lincoln). James writes for different age groups and is one of the few poets currently writing for younger children. He manages to write with depth, craft the poems and appeal to the younger age group. There are funny poems and thoughtful poems ('Crow', 'Sweet Meadow', 'So You Want to Build a Bear' or 'Sleep'), and many are great for performing.

This collection offers a marvellous hoard of different structures including haiku, free verse, rhyming poetry, some great shape poems which could be used as starting points for the children's own shape poems, and calligrams where the words and letters echo meaning. 'How Many Minibeasts?' is an invitation into creating collective nouns for different creatures. 'What is it?', 'Five Ways to Cross the...' and 'The Old Wood' are acrostics but in this poem the key word is hidden within the lines. This is called a 'mesostic'. 'Hey, Poem!' uses the actual font to suggest how the poem might be read aloud and to reinforce meaning. It would make an interesting poem for pairs to perform. The poem 'What the Mouse Said' made me want to go off and write a poem, listing all the sounds that a night creature might hear (eg 'What the cat/owl/fox/badger said...').

There is an interview at the end and a link to James's excellent website where you can find all his poetry books listed as well as his outstanding manuals for teachers about teaching and his latest, invaluable teaching guide, *Let's do Poetry in Primary Schools* (A&C Black).

The Puffin Book of Utterly Brilliant Poetry

Edited by Brian Patten (*Puffin*)

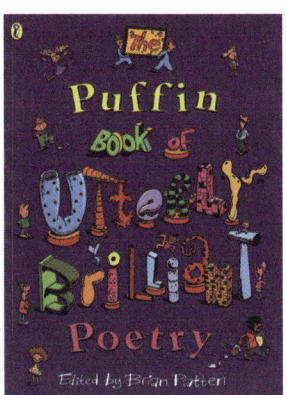

This playful anthology is a lively collection which introduces the class to a wide range of modern poets: Spike Milligan, Kit Wright, Michael Rosen, Charles Causley, Roger McGough, Benjamin Zephaniah, Brian Patten, Jackie Kay, John Agard and Allan Ahlberg. Each poet has space for about ten poems, is illustrated by a different artist and is introduced through an interview with Brian Patten. Ideally, you would have a few collections by each poet on hand so that when children enjoy a poet they can explore further, developing their own poetry tastes!

It would be interesting to get the children to discuss and write about each poet – what do they like/not like about each writer? This could lead towards drawing up their own 'desert island' list of their favourite ten poems as well as a class vote on the top three poets. Much of this work will hinge around experiencing the poems just for pleasure. It is worth building in two or three slots a day for sharing the poems so that every day one poem is read three times. This is because on the first reading the class may not have caught all the nuances, and revisiting gives the opportunity to notice different aspects of each poem. If children have access to the anthology then they will enjoy the illustrations. No one should miss Korky Paul's pictures for the marvellous 'Chocolate Cake'.

Part of the joy of this anthology is that the poems cover a full range of voices and styles, acting as an introduction to high quality poetry for younger juniors. Many of the poems are great fun but there are also more serious, memorable poems that are worth discussing. Roger McGough's 'The Sound Collector' and 'The Reader of this Poem' have both become standard models for children's writing in many schools. Charles Causley's 'My Mother Saw a Dancing Bear' is a classic and many of his poems deserve to be chorally performed, as do poems by Zephaniah and Ahlberg.

Year 4

Deep in the Green Wood

Wes Magee (*Caboodle Books*)

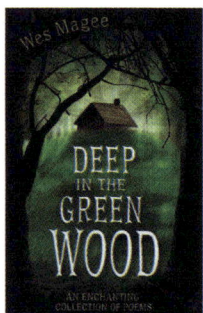

I first stumbled across Wes Magee's poetry as a young teacher. He is a master craftsman and this collection is rich in various styles and themes that children love. As a poet who has spent years working in schools, Wes has an eye for subjects that will entertain and the ability to craft the language so that it reads aloud perfectly. 'The Boneyard Rap', 'In the Castle of Doom' and 'The Witch's Brew' demand to be performed. 'City Sounds after Dark' would make a simple model for writing a list poem of sounds heard at night, though I would avoid using rhyme with children as they might write better without worrying about forcing a rhyme.

'Beach Quest' provides a powerful model for writing about any local setting or place visited on a class trip; use the format, *'What did we see/at Runswick Bay?'* and make lists of what was seen at a local setting. Turn each detail into a descriptive line. For instance, if you live in a town or city you might list the following: bus, lamppost, litter, shops. Take each one in turn and model how to develop the ideas by using description and, perhaps, a simile to build the picture for the reader without worrying about rhyme:

So, what did we see
In Stroud town centre?

A green village bus trundles by,
Slim lampposts watch from the sidelines,
Curled newspapers and flashy crisp packets scuttle along,
Shop windows are blank as winter ponds.

One of the first model poems that I used for writing is included in this collection: 'What is… the sun?' The poem is a very simple list of images to describe what the sun is like. I have used this many times and it never seems to fail. We begin by reading the poem collectively and then discuss each idea. Instead of writing about the sun, I use the moon – both the crescent moon and full moon. I begin by listing with the class possible similes, asking: *What does it look like or remind you of?* I often get the children to sketch the shape and turn it round so that the crescent can be seen upside down or sideways, as this prompts new ideas such as '*the moon is like – a bridge, an arc, a rainbow, a parachute, a moustache, a smile, a rocking chair*', etc. We discuss possible images as a class and then I use shared writing to show how to turn ideas into descriptive images:

The moon
Is a silver bridge,
A silent scythe
In the darkness,
A bone-white rainbow
Curved on its side,
A thin eyelash.

'The Family Clan' is a wonderful starting point for those children who want to rhyme. Start by making a list of names that are then turned into rhymes with place names, such as Jo from Plymouth Ho! I would start by using an atlas, as children will need to look for places that rhyme with names that they know. A version of this game is to make a list of place names and say what is happening there: *I was loud in Stroud,/ate snails in Wales,/saw green slime in Lyme!*

There are many poems here that are worth spending time with for discussion and deeper thought. I recently saw a class spend time with 'At the End of the School Day', teasing away at each verse, discussing the words and phrases and gradually building towards thinking about what the poem meant for them.

Hot Like Fire

Valerie Bloom (Bloomsbury)

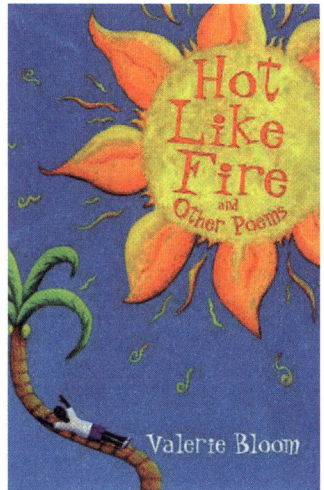

Hot Like Fire is a bumper collection as it also contains *The World is Sweet*. Valerie Bloom has for many years been performing and running workshops in schools. Originally from Jamaica, she was awarded an MBE for services to poetry in 2008. Caribbean life and culture are a strong thread through her poems, which are often written in patois as well as Standard English. If you look on the poetry archive website (www.poetryarchive.org) then you will not only find out more about Valerie but can also buy a CD or download audio of Valerie reading her poems. You can also see her performing poems on YouTube. This is essential, as part of her poetry is the music in her voice as she performs.

This collection is packed with poems to perform. 'Whose Dem Boots' can be chanted. Use a background sound of everyone slowly marching in time. Emphasise the final word, '*Huh!*' Ask: *Whose boots might be marching in this way and why is someone hiding?* I've heard Valerie perform this poem with an assembly full of children steadily marching and it was a very powerful political moment. There are wonderful poems to sing, perform and chant. Try letting the children work in groups. They have to select a poem to perform. Let them draw a text map to help them remember the lines and then decide how they are going to perform and what actions might help. Try playing the game 'Associations' in pairs just for the fun of bouncing words back and forth that seem to have an association. Read and talk through 'Seasons' and use it as a model for writing a short verse about each season using metaphors. Try using animals for the image. For instance, 'winter' might be a 'polar bear'.

Once you have decided this then just extend the idea, stating what the bear is doing:

Winter is a polar bear,
Prowling across the landscape,
Breathing snow and frost
Onto tree, branch and field,
Smothering city, town and forest
In splinters of white.

Read Val Bloom's poems about the weather as well as 'Seasons'. This poem was written in response, focussing on the cold wind blowing in the Winter.

Icy Breath
The wind crashes
with a piercing squeal
into the arched reeds
ripping the green
to pieces of thread.
Hair bellows out
as the wind cuts
into your face.
Fiercely,
it bends saplings.
Shredding leaves,
throwing fragments
into the air.

Tim Clapham 9 years

Year 4

Hello H₂O

John Agard (*Hodder*)

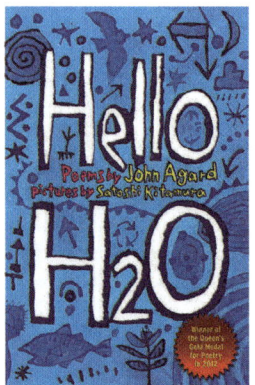

Gather a collection of John Agard's wonderful books for children so that plenty of his poetry is to hand, such as *The Rainmaker Danced* (Hodder), *Goldilocks on CCTV* (Frances Lincoln) and *Einstein, the Girl Who Hated Maths* (Hodder). He was born in Guyana, moved to England in the 1970s and has become a great force in both children's and adult's poetry, being awarded the Queen's Gold Medal for Poetry in 2012. His poems are often playful and this collection is built around a science theme. There are notes at the back to give some scientific information and background to the poems.

'Blowing Bubbles' is a poem that could be linked to just that. Blow some bubbles and then make a list of all the ideas that the children have about what the bubbles look like. Then use these to create poems, using a similar format to John's poem. The poem 'Recipe for a Chinese Floating Compass' could trigger the writing of other 'recipe' poems such as a recipe for a class outing, a good holiday, a great lesson. I love the idea of writing 'A Few Questions for the Tooth Fairy' which could be used imaginatively to ask questions of mythological creatures such as giants, ogres, elves, fairies and dragons. In the same vein, the poem 'Five Reasons Why I Would Volunteer for Outer Space' is a great writing idea. Ask: *Why would you volunteer to go to the moon?* 'Gifts for Earth's Atmosphere' could lead into a poem listing all the great things that are on earth naturally.

Our gifts for the earth include –
The silence of clouds,
the stillness of blue sky,
the tickle of warm wind,
cabbage white's flutter,
a fox's rusted fur...

The poem 'Under Galileo's Glass' would be an invitation to study natural objects using a magnifying lens or microscope if available. On the Internet, it is easy to locate close-up images of skin, insects, leaves, snowflakes that look like lunar landscapes and strange creatures. Children are always fascinated by these images. You could use the idea in the poem of transformation – under the lens what does each subject become?

A red admiral butterfly's wing
becomes a flamenco dancer's dress.

A blade of grass with dew
becomes a forest hung with gems.

Probably one of the most powerful water forces is a storm. This poem arose after a storm and in response to John Agard's Hello H₂O:

The storm

First a lash of lightning
licks the lilac cloud.

A muscular rein of lightning
punches the static ground.

The icy rain grips against the window
as it pours down on earth.

Richard, 9 years

Sensational!

Chosen by Roger McGough (*Macmillan*)

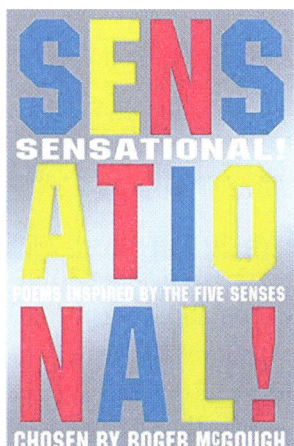

I chose this anthology because to be able to write well, and to live well, children need to be alert to their senses. When I was a teacher, I always began my writing curriculum each year by writing about the senses on the basis that for any descriptive writing, any place where we needed to get the reader imagining, we would have to recreate a real or imagined experience by using our senses so that the reader would be able to vividly see, touch, taste, hear or smell what was happening.

The book is packed with poems worth performing and discussing and is invaluable as a source for writing. The very first poem, 'The Magic of the Brain' is an ideal model. Work with the class to list memorable things that they have seen, heard, touched and tasted. These can be everyday things like a taxi, a thistle and commuters coming out of a station. Then take each idea and turn it into a descriptive line, using Jenny Joseph's format:

Such a sight I saw:
a black taxi crawling down the High Street,
a thistle growing out of a red brick wall
and commuters streaming out of Woodford Station,
blinking into sunlight.

Remember to encourage the use of 'naming' places as this may build a stronger picture for the reader and makes the writing sound realistic. Brian Patten's 'Not Only' makes a great performance poem, with children forming two lines and in turn repeating each line back at each other. Again, something similar may be written using the poem's pattern. Make a long list of everyday and special things to celebrate. In the same tone of celebrating the world, James Berry's 'Benediction' might be used as a model or Carol Ann Duffy's wonderful 'The Oldest Girl in the World' or Roger McGough's 'Joy at the Sound'.

Mandy Coe's 'Sensing Mother' is a poem to use sensitively for discussion and the classic 'Hide and Seek' by Vernon Scannell is worth loitering with for close discussion – and so, too, is his wonderful poem 'Nettles', which is rich with the imagery of war. You might get the class singing 'Who Has Seen the Wind?', and Hopkins's 'Pied Beauty' would be worth learning chorally, with time spent discussing carefully. Another classic, and one that is possibly more accessible, is John Clare's 'Pleasant Sounds', which could be used as a model for a list poem. It helps to gather a long list of 'sound words' for the class to use when writing, eg crunch, whistle, squeal, boom, rustle, whir, etc. Linda J Knauss's 'An 'Everything' Pizza' is plain silly but children will love writing their own versions.

I'd also want to get the class learning Eliot's 'Preludes' and looking at Edward Thomas's 'Digging' as preludes themselves to meeting these poets later on in the curriculum.

Year 5

Lost Magic

Brian Moses (*Macmillan*)

Brian and I were young teachers together. We used to spend hours talking about poetry, sharing writing ideas and discussing our own poems. At weekends, we would give poetry readings and performed with musicians, often setting poems to music. Brian has been working as a poet in schools for most of his career and has sold well over a million poetry books, reaching into almost every primary school in the country. This collection pulls together about 100 of his favourite poems. He is a tremendous writer for children and writes in a way that makes the poetry accessible and yet runs with the full range of emotions – exciting, rhythmic, scary, funny, political, eco-aware and deeply felt.

Brian has the knack of not letting the language obscure or become any sort of barrier to meaning. It is 'child-friendly' poetry; he has a flair for viewing the world as a resource for poems. For instance, there is a poem about the fact that goldfish lose their memory every four seconds and another about the fact that human beings swallow, on average, eight spiders in their lifetime during sleep! He has a great eye for the quirkiness in our lives and uses this material to alert children to the possibilities that life has to offer for writing.

Many of the poems lend themselves to modelling. 'Zoo of Winds' arose from an idea we discussed about 30 years ago about creating 'poetry zoos' and what might be in different cages. The desire to play with rhyme could be satisfied by using the same sort of structure as 'All the Things You Can Say to Places in the UK'. I've used 'Dragon's Wood' as a writing model – making lists of clues that a dragon or giant might be in the local area.

His classic 'Walking with my Iguana' is a YouTube hit and has been performed by children around the world. His slapstick poem 'Aliens Stole my Underpants' is also excellent for performance, as, too, are 'Shopping Trolley' and 'Monster Crazy'. Use percussion instruments as Brian does in his performances. By contrast, poems like 'Empty Places' are thoughtful. He also touches on the political and global with poems such as 'Names', 'Classroom Globe' and 'What are We Fighting For?'. His historical poems often draw on injustice and the madness of war. Supplement Brian's poems by downloading audio versions from the poetry archive, and use his BlogSpot for writing ideas.

The Magic Box

Kit Wright *(Macmillan)*

Virtually every primary teacher knows Kit Wright for his poem 'The Magic Box' which is a small but wonderful stroke of poetic genius. The poem acts as a catalyst for writing about the miraculous things that might be kept inside a magic box. It's a poem that almost every child will either meet in primary or secondary school. Somewhere along the line, an enthusiastic English teacher will be introducing it to them. Before shifting into writing, it is worth spending time looking carefully at the poem to think about how he creates the magical effects:

1. Alliteration ('*the tip of a tongue touching a tooth*').
2. Playful personification ('*a snowman with a rumbling belly*').
3. Last and first things ('*last joke and first smile*').
4. Impossible things and swaps ('*fifth season and cowboy on a broomstick*').
5. What your box is made from ('*ice and gold and steel*').
6. How you will travel in your box ('*surf*') and where you will go ('*yellow beach*').

I've used this poem, or the idea, from Nursery through to Higher Education. Here is the start of a class poem written with Year 3 children:

My Magic Box

I will put in my box a cold key opening cupboards of mystery,
a ten rupee note turning over and over,
a perfectly polished pebble,
a serious spike standing as tall as a tower that reaches the clouds,
a perky penguin sliding fast across the see through, slippery ice
and a tasty teaspoon touching a T-Rex's tooth!

I will put in my box
the hot fingers of the sun tickling the earth,
the moon's heartbeat pounding the night sky,
windows grinning at the chair stretching,
sand smiling all day,
doors snarling when rain falls
and dust swallowing the sea water.

I will put in my box
the last wish of a tooth fairy,
the last cry of a Chinese dragon,
the last croak of a multicoloured frog
and the last magic of an old crocodile driving a motorcycle.

I will put in my box
the first touch of a slippery goldfish,
the first question of a talking jellybean
and the first smile of a bored water hog.

I will put in my box
a thirteenth month,
a solid ocean,
a camouflaged mouse,
a flame-throwing monkey
and a spiked pillow.

I will put in my box
A shark with fins
and a horse with a mane
a goldfinch with antlers
and a deer with feathers.

My box is made from
silver haribos and gold wasps' nests
with a tiny grandma tap dancing on the lid
and emerging emeralds in the corners.
Its hinges are the horns of a charging bull.

I shall time travel in my box
on the boiling hot lava ocean
then end up at the fun fair of
Honkadookee's golden vultures.

But Kit is not a one-trick pony, as this marvellous collection demonstrates. He is a master craftsman. His poems cover a vast range of subjects. He can be very funny, as in 'Hugger Mugger', and in the next poem drop in something serious, as in 'The Song of the Whale'. I suspect that Kit constantly hears rhymes and indulges this passion in poems such as

Year 5

'Zoe's Ear-rings' which is a masterpiece of rhyming comedy that makes for a wonderful performance. Children love the comedy of his 'Dave Dirt' poems and those about 'Sergeant Brown's Parrot'.

I always used to teach my classes 'Red Boots On' which jogs along wonderfully and is an evocation of the joy found in wearing a new pair of red boots and walking through the snow. Perform with rhythm! Don't fight shy of more demanding and less obvious poems such as 'January Birth'. Read the poem and let it do its mysterious work. Read it several times during the day. Draw a chart of the children's favourite Kit Wright poems and end this stretch with any of these poets by getting the children to perform their favourite poems in small groups.

Juggling with Gerbils

Brian Patten (*Puffin*)

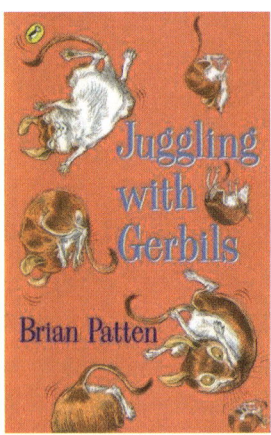

This little gem is marvellously illustrated by the great Chris Riddell. Check out Brian's poems on the poetry archive website (www.poetryarchive.org) where readings can be downloaded or an audio CD purchased. It would be lovely to read this collection alongside Brian's novel *Mr Moon's Last Case* (Puffin), his version of Beowulf, *Monster Slayer* (Barrington Stoke) or his novel about stories, *The Story Giant* (Harper Collins).

One of the original 'Liverpool Poets' alongside Adrian Henri and Roger McGough, Brian has devoted his life to poetry and performance. There is some silliness in this collection that will appeal to children, such as 'The Day I Got My Finger Stuck up My Nose', but in the main the poems offer a richer vein than slapstick. There is a film clip on the internet of Brian reading 'A Boat in the Snow' to a group of primary children and talking about his writing that is worth finding. The fine poem 'Geography Lesson' is one that every teacher should read and think about, taking its message to heart.

'Tiger Shadows' is a direct invitation to create your own version of the poem. *What animal would you become and what might happen?* 'In the Jungle Restaurant' provides a simple format to satisfy the desire to rhyme. 'The Inside of Things' also provides a simple, transferable pattern. This would sit well alongside 'Amulet' by Ted Hughes, which basically uses the same idea. 'One of the Difficulties of Writing a Poem' is an interesting way of looking at all the possibilities for word order. Challenge the class to play the same 'reordering' game with the following sentence:

Outside the rain fell like diamonds glittering on the tree's leaves.

'The Boy Who Broke Things' is a poem worth spending time with for deeper discussion.

Check out Brian's website as well (www.brianpatten.co.uk).

The Works 4

Chosen by Pie Corbett and Gaby Morgan (*Macmillan*)

The various meaty *Works* anthologies are worth having in school – all of them – because they provide a bank of thousands of poems. This collection is based around the sorts of things that children are interested in and it is packed with hundreds of modern poems that were originally selected for World Book Day publications by Gaby Morgan. We organised the collection around the letters of the alphabet so that you might take the poems under each letter and read them over several days. Vernon Scannell's poem 'Grannie' from this collection was used in the 2019 National Test – though no one asked me if I thought it was good idea!

As the anthology has so many poems, I'll choose a few of my favourites to mention. 'Rat It Up' by Adrian Mitchell is a great poem to perform, as, too, is Nick Toczek's 'The Dragon Who Ate Our School' and 'We Are Not Alone' by Paul Cookson. There are great film clips of performances of these poems on the internet, with Nick performing with a class and Paul performing to camera. Edward Lear's 'The Pobble Who Has No Toes' is a poem that every child should have met – but make sure you practise it aloud several times. John Whitworth's 'The Cheer-up Song' is a perfectly rhythmical read-aloud poem of great joy – and get the class joining in. Let the children know the story behind 'The Charge of the Light Brigade' and then learn this for performance chorally. I have a film clip of Year 4 children at Selby Primary performing this and it is thunderous in its energy, but draws to a quiet conclusion that leaves a lump in the throat.

Use Riad Nourallah's 'An Alphabet for the Planet' to create lists of things that we must protect. My own 'Secret Poem' came out of a writing workshop idea. The game is to take something abstract like a wish, dream, secret, lie or hope and list what you would need to make it, where you found it, what it can do and what might happen if you lost it. Here is the start of Matthew's poem when he was in Year 5:

My wish is made of –
the warmth from a scarf,
the purr of my cat Sugar
and the silence of clouds.

Make a big list with the children of possibilities for ingredients – which in essence could be anything that the imagination offers. Encourage them to use details, so instead of saying *'My wish is made from/my cat'*, think of a detail and write *'My wish is made from/a claw from my cat's paw'*. ■

Year 6

Collected Poems for Children

Charles Causley (*Macmillan*)

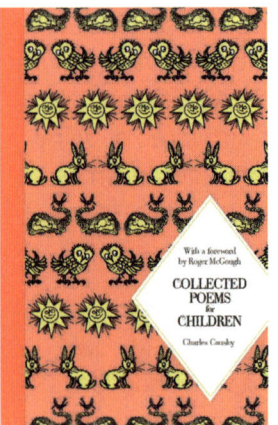

Charles Causley was a teacher for much of his life. He wrote a huge body of work for both children and adults and was recognised as the master of more formal writing, especially memorable ballads. Many of his poems sound like ancient songs or traditional folk songs. They seem timeless and certainly not tied into any modern trend. The poems are rooted in his home county of Cornwall, and in traditional tales and traditions, and are capable of being both light and profound. They are the sorts of poem that echo in the mind long after reading.

Here are great poems that every child should know and at some point have the chance to learn orally and chorally perform. Sadly, since Causley wrote 'Timothy Winters' the theme of child poverty remains in our society. 'Colonel Fazakerly', 'What Has Happened to Lulu?', 'I Saw a Jolly Hunter', 'My Mother Saw a Dancing Bear' and '"Quack," said the Billy-goat' are all great poems for differing reasons.

Because the poems rely so much upon their musicality, it is important to read them through before performing in the classroom. So much of the meaning is in the harmony with the musicality such that a hesitant reading can spoil the joy. Look at 'Tabitha Tupper' and you can see how a smooth reading is required so that it jogs along full of spritely wit.

This collection is rich with Charles Causley's own fanciful, mythological world rooted in the past but creating the sorts of poem that will last forever. A word of warning – children cannot possibly master writing ballads. These are poems to perform, to enjoy, to discuss, to wonder about and perhaps write in response. But the structures are too demanding to act as direct models for children's own writing. Causley was a genius and a genuine craftsman. The book is wonderfully illustrated by John Lawrence.

Collected Poems for Children

Ted Hughes (*Faber & Faber*)

Ted Hughes was a Poet Laureate. He wrote wonderfully for children and adults and this collected works brings together some of the finest poetry written for children at the end of the last century. The collection begins with poems for younger children and makes its way through to more demanding poetry that sets the groundwork for ongoing poetic experience at Key Stage 3. Raymond Briggs, of 'The Snowman' fame affectionately illustrates the volume.

'The Mermaid's Purse' and 'The Cat and the Cuckoo' find Ted Hughes writing for much younger children, which is probably not his most secure territory. 'Meet My Folks' was an early publication of poems about families and has some gems. 'Nessie' is an extended story poem. 'Moon Whales and Other Moon Poems' is an extraordinary set of poems based on Hughes' invention of an imaginary moon. Here he is flexing his writing powers to create a new world.

'Under the North Star' finds Ted Hughes on home territory with an astonishing group of poems about animals. I would introduce each poem with an image or film clip of the specific creature. Children do not have to understand everything to feel the vivid power of the poems that capture the spirit of the animals. The first poem in this collection, 'Amulet', is an ideal model for writing. Here is part of Ralph's poem, written when he was in Year 6, in response:

Inside the snow flake's bite of cold
Is a whispering wind of wilderness.

Inside the glittered, scattered snow
is a song of the thaw.

Inside the last leaf of snow
Is a wish of cold winter's end.

The anthology contains the animal poems from 'What is the Truth?' and ends with the full collection of 'Season Songs'. 'The Warm and the Cold' is the sort of poem that Year 6 children should be reading aloud, discussing, annotating and enjoying. The animal poems are based around close observation. Much of Hughes' writing literally began with him studying closely an insect or animal *in situ*, making notes. He writes about this in *Poetry in the Making*, which is the best book there is on helping children to write powerfully. The opening chapter has much to say about the need to observe carefully and gives plenty of useful hints for the teacher of writing, such as getting the children to write silently, meditatively and at pace based on a first-hand experience.

New and Collected Poems for Children

Carol Ann Duffy (*Faber & Faber*)

This collection was published when Carol Ann Duffy was Poet Laureate and brings together her four collections written for children. The poems vary from the daft, the surreal and the elegant through to those that seem to offer an exuberant playfulness with words and ideas. 'The Birds, the Fish and the Insects' and 'The Fruits, the Vegetables, the Flowers and the Trees' are both good examples of just playing with an idea and seeing how far it can run. It also reminds me of why I give time limits to children when they are writing in order to avoid the danger of overextending an idea! 'No Stone Unturned' works in the same way and acts as a great model for writing.

There are plenty of poems to use as catalysts for writing. 'Don't Be Scared' is a list of metaphors for the dark. 'His Nine Sympathies' might lead into thinking about whom we might feel sympathetic towards and using the same simple pattern to write. 'The Alphabet' could use the same structure, keeping the first word in each line but altering the examples so that the first line might shift to:

Aye! to rain after weeks of sun and scorched earth.

'Perhaps' provides more of a challenge as a model. Work with the class to create images and think imaginatively about what different things might they become or do. 'The Look' is also more of a challenge, but one that children enjoy. Make long lists of things to write about and then the class just has to decide what each one is 'the look of'.

The poem 'Bad Number' offers a simple form for rhyming that many children enjoy, and in this case will work, as the poem is based on a simple list format. Let the children choose their own bad or good numbers and model how to write a simple rhyming couplet:

33 swallows on a wire.
33 children in a choir.

Many of the poems use rhyme playfully, but be wary of this when children write as it usually leads into nonsense. Children need tight structures for rhyme, usually where the end result is just language play. In 'Opposites' the surreal nonsense element means that rhyme might work, but some children may prefer to write their lists without rhyme, which is fine.

Children will meet Carol Ann Duffy's poetry at secondary school so this early introduction will mean that her poetic quirkiness is already part of their poetic memory.

Year 6

The Works Key Stage 2

Chosen by Pie Corbett (*Macmillan*)

In this anthology I brought together a wide variety of poems that I would want to have with me if I was teaching in Key Stage 2. The range includes classic and modern poems ranging from William Blake's 'The Tyger' through to Philip Gross's 'Curious Craft'. At the back of the book, I have suggested in which year group the different poems might be experienced and drawn upon for teaching. This could act as a basic spine, poem-by-poem, enriched by the use of the poet studies as suggested in the spine.

By Year 6, children need to be getting their teeth into the great poems such as 'Jabberwocky', 'The Tyger', 'The Listeners', 'The Highwayman' and 'Kubla Khan', as well as some Shakespeare. Adrian Mitchell's poem 'Yes' makes a great model for rhyming couplets but is also very powerful when performed. James Kirkup's 'The Visitor' also makes an excellent performance piece.

The anthology starts with an alphabet and then a counting poem, both of which could be used as a model for writing. In the past, I have used 'The Magical Mouse' as a basis for creating amazing creatures. 'Work on Stone' and 'The Unwritten' are also both ideal for stimulating ideas. Ask: *What might lie trapped inside a snowflake or a star or a tree?* Both poems by Edward Thomas go together well. Let the children discuss in small groups and show them how to read carefully, word by word, to tease away at what each poem means for them. William Blake's poems 'The Sick Rose', 'The Quarrel' and 'A Poison Tree' also go together and complement each other. Give time to bigger poems such as Vernon Scannell's 'The Apple-raid', 'The Bully Asleep' and 'High Dive'.

'Six Ways of Looking at a Pond' was written by Kathryn Hoblin in Year 5. Make a list of possible subjects – tree, cloud, moon, raindrop, etc. To create the poem, write a new image or idea for each number. 'To Make a Prairie' and 'Making the Countryside' introduce the notion of writing a poem in the form of a recipe such as 'How to have a great summer holiday'. There are some well-known model poems such as 'The Magic Box' and my own poem 'Wings', which I wrote sitting on top of the Downs in East Sussex.